CORN[illegible]
COUNTRY RECIPES

COMPILED BY
SARAH GOMAR

Published by Ravette Books Limited
3 Glenside Estate, Star Road
Partridge Green, Horsham,
Sussex RH13 8RA
(0403) 710392

Production: Oval Projects Ltd.
Cover design: Jim Wire
Typesetting: Repro-type
Printing & binding: Nørhaven AS

All recipes are given in Imperial and Metric weights and measures. Where measurments are given in 'cups', these are American cups, holding 8 fluid ounces.

The recipes contained in this book are traditional and many have been compiled from archival sources. Every effort has been made to ensure that the recipes are correct.

RECIPES

SOUPS and BEGINNINGS

Creamy Egg Mayonnaise 1
Saffron Soup 2
Kidney Soup 3
Cornish Farm Broth with Suet Dumplings 4
Conger Eel Soup 6
Mackerel Paté 7

FISH

Marinated Mackerel 8
Baked Mackerel with Gooseberry Sauce 9
Limpets 10
Spider Crab Supper 11
Scrowled Pilchards 11
Fish Balls 12
Red Mullet Parcels 13
Roast Bream 14

POULTRY and MEAT

Chicken Cream 15
Roast Herby Chicken with Cider Sauce 16
Cottage Pie 17

Sausage or Corn Beef Fritters 18
Toad-in-the-Hole 19
Beef Stewed in Beer with Potato Topping 20
Blanquette of Veal 22
Pork Jelly 24
Roast Pork and Vegetable Bake 25
Pork Cobbler 26

SAVOURY PIES and PASTIES

Star-Gazey Pie 28
Salmon Pie 30
Trout Pie 32
Squab Pie 33
Creamy Chicken, Ham and Leek Pie 34
Rabbit Pie 36
Mutton and Apple Pie 37
Cornish Pasties 38
Meat Pasty 39
Herby Pasty 40
Likky Pasty 41

BREAKFAST or HIGH TEA

Ham Toast 42
Buttered Eggs 43
Potato Cakes 44
Broccoli and Bacon Supper Dish 45

VEGETABLES

Broccoli or Cauliflower in Cheese Sauce 46
Cucumber in Vinegar 47
Buttered Turnips 47

PUDDINGS

Blackberry and Apple Pancakes 48
Cornish Mince Pies 50
Spicy Apple Pie 52
Plum Pudding 53
Gingerbread Pudding 54
Aunt Nellie's Treacle Pudding 55
Figgie 'obbin 56
Baked Figgy Pudding 57
To Make a Tansey 58
Cornish Burnt Cream 59
Cornish Junket 60

SUNDRIES

Cornish Clotted Cream 61

CAKES, SCONES and CREAM

Black Cake 62
Cornish Heavy Cake 65

Sly Cakes	66
Cornish Splits	67
Fairings	68
Cornish Gingerbread	69
Potato Cakes for Tea	70
Porter Cake	71
Simnel Cake	72

PRESERVES and SAUCES

Strawberry Jam	74
Apple and Date Chutney	75
Fennel Sauce	76
Cider Sauce	77
Blackberry Syrup	78

DRINKS

Brandy and Rhubarb Cordial	79
Mrs Boilay's Beef Tea	80
Eggy'ot	81
Mahogany	81
Metheglin or Spiced Mead	82
Spruce	83

AN OLD REMEDY

The Most Admirable Beauty Wash that was ever known	84

CORNWALL

The dramatic county of Cornwall in the extreme south west of the country, is almost entirely surrounded by sea. Dominated by water, the Cornish were great seafarers and have for centuries relied heavily upon fishing as well as mixed farming for much of their income and foodstuffs.

Hake, boiled and fried; pilchards, 'scrowled marinated and salted'; mackerel, conger, whiting and fish of other varieties with big meaty potatoes, formed the staple meals varied by Cornish pasties and substantial pies.

Almost the only sweet for the table of the working man was treacle — dark coloured and thick, and very different from the 'golden syrup' of the present day.

Fishing was an industry that involved not only the fishermen but the community as a whole. When a large fish catch was landed, locals would help to bring the catch ashore, then sort, clean and sometimes preserve the fish.

Pilchards salted in casks and exported from Cornwall were known in Italy as 'fairmaids'. In Cornwall itself, Jousters (Cornish fish sellers) carried large baskets on their backs full of fish to sell at local farms and villages.

The pasty is probably the most famous Cornish dish and is eaten not only in Cornwall but throughout the country as a quick, nourishing meal. It is reported that Clayworkers took pasties up to two foot long to work and washed them down with strong tea — and then suffered from indigestion.

Pies have been popular in Cornwall long before the famous pasty. Pies such as Muggety pie (made with sheep's pluck or pig's intestine and covered with currants, sugar, spice and parsley), Star-gazey pie (cooked with the fish whole and their heads protruding through the pastry top), and Squab pie, have been eaten for generations, and it is said that the devil would not venture into Cornwall for fear they might put him in a pie.

The social and historical importance of the pie throughout England is emphasised by its repeated use in many of the well known old nursery rhymes such as Georgie-Porgie Pudding and Pie, Little Jack Horner and Sing a Song of Sixpence. The four and twenty black birds in that pie began to sing when the pie was opened which records the fact that all sorts of things used to be put in a pie, and some of them while still alive.

The Cornish bake special cakes, buns and biscuits for all occasions. Tea-treats, religious gatherings, are still held in towns and villages throughout Cornwall. They are now as then, occasions for all the family with usually a procession and a band playing. The children sit at trestle tables, and feast on specially baked saffron tea-treat buns.

A special annual event was held at Pentille Castle, Pillaton, each July to mark the end of cherry picking season. The local school children were invited to the castle where there would be games and entertainment followed by a cherry pie feast at which the children would eat as much pie as they could manage.

Markets, fairs and regattas are an important and colourful part of Cornwall's history. Special ginger biscuits, known as 'fairings', were baked and sold at many of these occasions.

Farmers and workmen in Cornwall still break from work for a bun and tea, known as 'croust' in west Cornwall and 'crib' in mid-Cornwall. In former times especially during the Harvest, croust or crib time would be a much larger and more important occasion with women and children bringing picnic baskets to the fields for the labourers and drinks such as Spruce.

Grovey cake was made after pig killing time. The 'groves', the dried brown fat pieces left after the fat had been rendered down to lard, were made into a cake with barley flour and salt, baked, cut into squares and served hot. Barley flour was more often used in baking than the more expensive wheat flour.

Other traditional Cornish dishes include potato cakes, saffron cake, heavy cake and figgie 'obbin. Saffron cakes can still be brought in bakers' shops for although saffron has become less popular in other counties it is still used in Cornwall to add colour and to impart a subtle flavour to food.

With a good climate for soft fruits like black cherries and strawberries, plentiful apple, plum and pear orchards, and high quality dairy produce crowned by the famed clotted cream, Cornwall provides its people and its visitors with a rich choice.

‘Pastry rolled out like a plate,
Piled with ‘turmut, tates and mate’,
Doubled up and baked like fate,
That’s a Cornish Pasty.’

Traditional

CREAMY EGG MAYONNAISE Serves 4

A popular beginning to a summer meal in many counties, this Cornish version has cream added to the mayonnaise.

For the mayonnaise - makes ½ pint:
2 egg yolks
½ teaspoon salt or to taste
½ teaspoon dry mustard
1 tablespoon lemon juice or white wine vinegar
6 fl oz (175 ml/ ¾ cup) olive oil
2 tablespoons double cream

For the eggs:
4 eggs
Anchovy fillets
Lettuce to garnish

To make the mayonnaise:

Mix the egg yolks with the salt and mustard.

Stir in the lemon juice or vinegar until smooth.

Add the oil to the egg mixture one drop at a time.

Beat the mixture thoroughly between each addition.

When the mixture begins to thicken, the oil can be added more quickly, whisking continuously.

Stir in the cream.

To prepare the eggs:

Boil the eggs for 10 minutes.

Cool them under cold running water before shelling.

Cut each egg in half. Arrange on a bed of lettuce.

Coat each egg with mayonnaise and garnish with anchovy fillets.

SAFFRON SOUP

Serves 4

This soup dates from at least the 14th Century. Saffron was very popular in medieval cooking and has been used extensively in Cornwall for generations.

2 onions
2 potatoes
1½ pints (900 ml/ 3¾ cups) milk
¼ teaspoon saffron
A little warm water
Salt and pepper
3 oz (75 g) cheese
2 tablespoons double cream

Peel and chop the potatoes and onions.

Put in a saucepan and add the milk.

Cook for 20 minutes or until the vegetables are soft.

Rub through a sieve or blend in the electric mixer.

Return the thickened liquid to the saucepan.

Mix the saffron in a little warm water and stir into the soup with salt and pepper to taste.

Grate the cheese and add to the soup.

Cook, stirring constantly, until the cheese melts.

Swirl in the cream before serving.

Hay rick

KIDNEY SOUP

Serves 4

Lambs' kidneys have traditionally been popular in Cornish dishes.

8 oz (225 g) lamb's kidney
Seasoned flour
4 oz (100 g) bacon
1 onion
Fat for frying
2 pints (1.15 litres/ 4 cups) brown stock
A bouquet garni sachet
Salt and pepper
About 2 oz (50 g) flour for thickening
A little milk
2 tablespoons Cornish clotted or double cream

Skin and core the kidney and cut up into slices.

Roll the kidney pieces in the seasoned flour.

Remove the rind from the bacon and cut into small pieces.

Peel and chop the onion.

Heat the fat in a thick saucepan.

Fry the kidney, bacon and onion lightly.

Drain off the fat, and gradually stir in the stock.

Add the bouquet garni and season with salt and pepper.

Bring to the boil and simmer for at least 1 hour.

Skim off any fat and remove the bouquet garni sachet.

When the kidney is tender, blend the flour with a little milk and hot soup.

Stir this into the soup and bring to the boil to thicken.

Swirl the cream into the soup just before serving and do not allow the soup to boil again after it has been added.

CORNISH FARM BROTH WITH SUET DUMPLINGS

Serves 4

For the broth:
4 oz (100 g) dried spilt peas
1 lb (450 g) boiling beef, salted brisket or silverside
2 pints (1.15 litres/ 4 cups) stock or water
2 large carrots
1 onion
1 leek
2 oz (50 g) turnip
A few cauliflower sprigs
Salt and pepper
4 suet dumplings

For the suet dumplings:
1½ oz (40 g) shredded suet
3 oz (75 g) plain flour
Salt
Water or milk to mix

To make the broth:

Soak the dried split peas overnight in cold water.

Drain and put with the meat in a large saucepan.

Cover with the stock or water.

Bring to the boil and simmer for 1½ hours.

Peel and chop the carrots, onion and turnip.

Wash and chop the leek and break the cauliflower into florets.

Add the vegetables to the soup, season with salt and pepper, and continue cooking for about 45 minutes.

To make the dumplings:

Put the shredded suet, flour and salt into a bowl.

Mix with a little water or milk to a soft dough.

Form with the hands into small balls rolling each one in flour.

Drop the dumplings into the simmering broth and continue cooking for a further 20 minutes or until the dumplings are light and fluffy and the meat and vegetables are cooked.

Remove the boiled beef, which can be served sliced with boiled potatoes and vegetables as a hot meal after the soup, or cold with salad at another time.

Serve the broth in bowls with the dumplings.

CONGER EEL SOUP

Serves 6

The conger eel is a sea fish, which is often caught off the Cornish coast. Brown on top and silver underneath it can grow up to 8 feet long, so young ones, which are cooked like freshwater eels are best for this recipe.

1 lb (450 g) eels
1½ oz (40 g) butter or margarine
2 oz (50 g) flour
2½ pints (1.4 litres/ 5 cups) white stock, preferably fish
1 bouquet garni
1 onion
A little powdered mace
Salt and pepper
6 peppercorns
A little parsley for garnish

Remove the heads and tails of the eel or eels.

Soak in cold salted water for 20 minutes then remove and pull off the skin.

Cut the eel into small cutlets.

Melt the fat in a saucepan, put in the sliced eel, and fry gently until lightly brown.

Remove the fish.

Stir in the flour to make roux, and cook stirring continuously for a few minutes.

Gradually add the fish stock, onion, bouquet garni, herbs and seasoning and the eels.

Bring to the boil and simmer gently for about 40 minutes or until the fish is tender.

Strain the soup.

Take the fish off the bones and flake.

Add the flaked fish to the soup.

Serve garnished with finely chopped parsley.

MACKEREL PATÉ

Serves 4

1 smoked mackerel
6 oz (175 g) butter or margarine
4 oz (100 g) cheese
1 tablespoon lemon juice
Salt and pepper

Skin the mackerel and remove any bones.

Flake the fish into a bowl.

Melt the fat and add to the fish.

Allow to cool.

Grate the cheese finely.

Mix the cheese, lemon juice and seasoning with the fish to taste.

Either pound to a paste with a pestle and mortar or blend in a liquidiser.

Pack into a paté dish.

Serve with hot toast.

Mackarel Smack.

MARINATED MACKEREL

Serves 4

Historically large shoals of mackerel were found off the Cornish coast, and it has always been popular in Cornish cookery. To eat a fish straight from the sea is a great treat. This delicious fish is sometimes called 'The poor man's trout' and can be cooked in the same ways - grilled, fried, or baked. A really fresh mackerel will be almost stiff, bright in colour and have clear eyes. A round oily fish with attractive bluish black markings on its back, rich in protein and vitamins, it is in season from July to October.

4 mackerel
2 small onions
1 oz (25 g) parsley
2 bay leaves
6 cloves
6 peppercorns
1 blade of mace
Salt and pepper
About ¾ pint (450 ml/ 2 cups) vinegar

Prepare and wash the mackerel and lay them in an ovenproof dish.

Peel and finely chop the onions, parsley and bay leaves.

Sprinkle the onion, parsley and bay leaves together with the cloves, peppercorn and mace over the fish.

Season with salt and pepper.

Add sufficient vinegar to cover the fish well.

Bake in a moderate oven for 45 minutes or until the fish is tender.

Arrange on a serving dish, strain the cooking liquid and pour it over the fish.

Leave to marinate for several hours before serving.

Oven: 350°F/180°C Gas Mark 4

BAKED MACKEREL WITH GOOSEBERRY SAUCE

Serves 4

The taste for mackerel with gooseberry sauce is said to date back to the Norman Conquest, when it was brought over from France, and is a favourite in Cornwall. The taut, tangy flavour of the gooseberries cuts the oilyness of the fish.

4 mackerel
Salt and pepper
2 oz (50 g) butter

For the gooseberry sauce:
½ lb (225 g) gooseberries
1 oz (25 g) sugar
1 oz (25 g) butter
2 sprigs of parsley

Cut and clean the mackerel.

Arrange the fish in a greased ovenproof dish.

Season well with salt and pepper.

Dot with butter and cover the dish with foil.

Bake in a moderate oven for 30 minutes or until the fish are tender.

Carefully split each cooked fish down the back and remove the bone. Arrange on a serving dish and keep hot.

To make the gooseberry sauce:

Top and tail the gooseberries.

Put in a saucepan and add the sugar and a little water.

Cook gently until tender.

Sieve the fruit or liquidise in an electric blender.

Reheat gently and stir in the butter and chopped parsley.

Pour over the fish and serve hot.

Oven: 350°F/180°C Gas Mark 4

LIMPETS

Serves 2

Limpets, which cling tightly to the rocks around the coast, are small shelled molluscs.

They can be served like cockles, as in this recipe, fried or used in soups. They can also be substituted for mussels in sauces or other dishes.

About 1 pint (600 ml/ 2½ cups) limpets
Salted water
A little vinegar
Pepper to taste

Wash the limpets well to get rid of any sand.

Put in a basin of lightly salted water and soak for 2 hours.

Drain.

Put the limpets in a saucepan and cover with cold water.

Bring to the boil and cook until the limpets will slip easily out of the shells.

Rinse in cold water.

Pick out of the shells with a pin if necessary.

Serve cold, sprinkled with vinegar and pepper to taste.

SCROWLED PILCHARDS

Serves 4

A scrowler is a Cornish grid iron. It has a long handle and was used to cook the fish over an open fire.

8 pilchards
Salt and pepper
A little lemon juice

Clean the fish.

Split each fish completely.

Season well and sprinkle with a little lemon juice.

Grease a baking tray and cook the fish under a hot grill.

Allow about 3-5 minutes each side.

SPIDER CRAB SUPPER

Serves 2

Spider crabs are found round the Cornish coast. They are similiar to other crabs. For family crab suppers in Cornwall it was usual to have several separate bowls in the middle of the table.

1 boiled crab
Salt and pepper
Lemon juice
1 tablespoon of oil
1 tablespoon of white wine vinegar
A little made mustard (optional)

Remove all the meat from the crab.

Mix together with the salt and pepper, lemon juice, oil, vinegar and mustard.

Pile into a serving bowl, and eat with brown bread and butter.

FISH BALLS

Serves 4

A very old handwritten recipe for fried breaded fish.

1 lb (450 g) cod or haddock
A little milk for cooking
6 oz (175 g) breadcrumbs
A little finely chopped parsley
2 eggs, beaten
Salt and pepper
Fat or vegetable oil for frying
Lemon slices

Cook the fish in a little milk and water for about 15 minutes or until the fish is tender.

Remove the skin and bones and cut the fish into 1½ inch pieces.

Mix the breadcrumbs with the parsley, salt and pepper.

Add the beaten egg to moisten the mixture.

Take a piece of fish and form it into a ball.

Dip it into the breadcrumb mixture and roll it until it is well covered.

Repeat this method until all the fish pieces are covered with breadcrumbs.

Heat the cooking fat in a pan and cook the fish pieces over a medium heat until a golden brown.

Serve with slices of lemon.

RED MULLET PARCELS

Serves 4

This attractive salt water fish, is abundant around the coast of Cornwall. Red Mullet has a good flavour and is best baked or grilled. The liver of the fish is a great delicacy.

4 mullets
2 oz (50 g) parsley
4 shallots
Salt and pepper
A little lemon juice

Wash the fish carefully, and remove the gills. However, leave the liver intact to enhance the flavour.

Peel and finely chop the shallots.

Finely chop the parsley.

Mix the parsley, shallots and seasoning with a little lemon juice.

Place each fish on a piece of greased ovenproof paper or foil, large enough to wrap it in.

Put some herby mixture over each fish.

Wrap up and seal each parcel.

Place the fish parcels on a baking sheet.

Bake in a moderate oven for 15-20 minutes.

Oven: 375°F/190°C Gas Mark 5

ROAST BREAM

Serves 4

Sea Bream has white delicate flesh; fresh-water bream is much coarser in texture. Both the sea and fresh water fish are best baked with a savoury stuffing, but they can also be boiled, fried or grilled.

1 large or 2 small bream
1 oz (25 g) butter

For the stuffing:
2 oz (50 g) shredded suet
4 oz (100 g) breadcrumbs
1 oz (25 g) parsley
A pinch of salt
Milk to mix

To make the stuffing:

Chop the parsley finely.

Mix the suet, salt, breadcrumbs and parsley together.

Stir in sufficient milk to bind the the ingredients to a firm dough.

To prepare the fish:

Clean and remove the scales from the fish.

Fill the fish with the stuffing.

Put the fish into an ovenproof dish.

Dot with the butter.

Bake in a moderate oven for 20-25 minutes until golden brown.

Baste, adding more butter if required from time to time during cooking.

Oven: 350°F/180°C Gas Mark 4

CHICKEN CREAM

Serves 3-4

A 19th century recipe, served with hot buttered toast, which makes a delicious beginning to a meal.

8 oz (225 g) cooked minced chicken
2 tablespoons fresh breadcrumbs
2 tablespoons cream
1 egg, beaten
A little nutmeg
Slices of lemon to garnish

Mix the chicken and breadcrumbs together thoroughly.

Bind with the beaten egg.

Add the cream and beat to a smooth paste.

Add a little nutmeg to taste.

Butter a heatproof dish.

Put in the chicken mixture.

Cover with a cloth and tie securely.

Steam for half an hour.

Serve garnished with lemon.

ROAST HERBY CHICKEN WITH CIDER SAUCE

1 roasting chicken - about 3-3½ lb (1.5 kg - 1.6 kg)
1 large onion
5 oz (150 g) butter
3 oz (75 g) fresh breadcrumbs
1 oz (25 g) fresh sage
1 oz (25 g) fresh rosemary
1 oz (25 g) fresh thyme
1 egg beaten
A little lemon juice
Salt and pepper

Finely chop the sage, rosemary and thyme.

Finely chop the onion.

Melt 3 oz (75 g) butter in a pan and lightly fry the onion for a few moments.

Remove from the heat and mix with the breadcrumbs and herbs.

Bind together with the egg and a little lemon juice.

Season with salt and pepper.

Prepare the bird in the usual way and stuff with the herb mixture.

Cut up the remaining butter and spread over the bird.

Place in a roasting tin and cover with foil.

Cook for 1-1½ hours, basting frequently.

Remove the foil and allow the bird to brown for about 15 minutes before the end of cooking.

If the joints pull away easily from the body, the bird is cooked.

Put the chicken on a serving plate and keep warm.

Serve with Cider sauce (see recipe).

COTTAGE PIE

Serves 4

Cottage Pie is traditional in British cooking and is very popular in Cornwall. It is best made with freshly minced beef, but left-over meat is frequently used up in this dish.

1 onion
1 lb (450 g) minced beef
Oil for frying
1 tablespoon flour
¼ pint (150 ml/ ⅔ cup) brown stock
1 tablespoon tomato purée
1 tablespoon red wine (optional)
A pinch of marjoram
Salt and pepper
1 lb (450 g) cooked, mashed potatoes
1 oz (25 g) grated Cheddar cheese

Peel and chop the onion.

Fry the minced beef and onion in the hot fat until brown.

Stir in the flour and add the stock.

Mix in the herbs, purée, wine and salt and pepper to taste.

Put the meat mixture into an ovenproof dish.

Cover with mashed potatoes, fluffing up the top with a fork.

Bake in a moderate oven for about 40 minutes.

Sprinkle the top with grated cheese and brown under a hot grill before serving.

Oven: 350°F/180°C Gas Mark 4

Cottage

SAUSAGE OR CORN BEEF FRITTERS

Serves 12

A substantial and popular treat for high tea or a light supper, this sausage was served with fried bacon, potatoes and tomatoes.

If preferred thick slices of corned beef may be used in place of sausage meat.

1 lb (450 g) sausagemeat
Fat for frying

For the batter:
8 oz (225 g) plain flour
A pinch of salt
2 eggs
½ pint (300 ml/ 1¼ cups) milk

To make the batter:

Sieve the flour and salt into a basin.

Make a well in the centre.

Add the eggs one at a time, and gradually mix in the milk drawing in the flour working from the centre outwards.

Beat until smooth.

The batter can be mixed altogether in a liquidiser, if preferred.

To make the fritters:

Put the sausage meat into a frying pan and cook very gently, stirring occasionally for about 5 minutes.

Put the meat on a floured board, and form into small cakes.

Dip the meat cakes into the batter so that they are well coated.

Deep fry in hot fat for about 5 minutes until golden brown.

Drain well.

TOAD-IN-THE-HOLE

Serves 4

A traditional Toad-in-the-Hole is made with pieces of steak. The Cornish version includes replacing the batter with a mixture of mashed potato, suet and flour.

1 lb (450 g) frying steak
1 oz (25 g) lard or dripping
1 lb (450 g) mashed potatoes made with 1 oz (25 g) butter and a little milk
3 oz (75 g) suet
1 oz (25 g) flour
1 egg, beaten
Salt and pepper

Cut the steak into slices and fry in the hot fat for a few minutes.

Mix the mashed potatoes, suet and flour together.

Add the beaten egg to bind together.

Season with salt and pepper and knead to a stiff dough.

Roll out on a floured surface to about 1 inch (2.5 cm) thick.

Put the pieces of meat into the mixture.

Place in a greased baking tin and bake in a moderate oven until golden brown.

Sausages can be cut up and put in the potato mixture in place of the steak.

Oven: 375°F/190°C Gas Mark 5

Jolly Butcher

BEEF STEWED IN BEER WITH POTATO TOPPING

Serves 4

1 lb (450 g) stewing steak
2 oz (50 g) seasoned flour
1 lb (450 g) onions
2 carrots
Oil for frying
Salt and pepper
Bay leaf
1 lb (450 g) potatoes
1 oz (25 g) lard or dripping
½ pint (300 ml/ 1¼ cups) beef stock
½ pint (300 ml/ 1¼ cups) beer

Trim the meat and cut into neat 1 inch (2.5 cm) chunks.

Roll in the seasoned flour.

Peel and chop the onions and carrots.

Heat the oil until hot in a frying pan.

Fry the onions until soft. Drain and put on one side.

Fry the beef until golden brown on all sides.

Put the beef and vegetables in layers in ovenproof dish, seasoning each layer with salt and pepper.

Mix the beef stock with the beer and pour over the meat and vegetables.

Add the bay leaf.

Peel and slice the potatoes.

Put a layer of overlapping potato slices on top of the stew.

Brush the top with melted lard or dripping.

Cover the dish with a lid.

Cook in a moderate oven for 1½ hours or until the meat and potatoes are tender.

Remove the lid and brown the potatoes in a hot oven for 20 minutes.

Take out the bay leaf before serving.

Oven: 350°F/180°C Gas Mark 4
Increase to: 400°F/200°C Gas Mark 6

BLANQUETTE OF VEAL Serves 4

Cold cooked veal may be used in this dish, in which case the meat can be cut up and put straight into the sauce.

1 lb (450 g) veal
½ lb (225 g) onions
Bouquet garni
White stock to cover

For the sauce:
2 oz (50 g) butter
2 oz (50 g) plain flour
1 pint (600 ml/ 2½ cups) milk or ½ pint (300 ml/ 1¼ cups) milk and ½ pint (300 ml/ 1¼ cups) stock
Salt and pepper
A pinch of mace
2 oz (50 g) single cream
The juice of half a lemon
4 oz (100 g) mushrooms

To garnish:
Chopped parsley
Small pieces of toast

To cook the veal:

Cut up the veal into small pieces.

Peel and chop the onions.

Put the meat and onions in a saucepan with sufficient stock to cover.

Add the bouquet garni.

Bring to the boil and simmer gently for about 1 hour or until the veal is tender.

Strain and reserve the meat, and the stock if using stock in the sauce.

To make the sauce:

Melt the butter or margarine in a saucepan.

Stir in the flour to make a roux.

Cook for a minute or two over a low heat, still stirring gradually add the milk or milk and stock.

Bring to the boil and then simmer, stirring until the sauce thickens.

Season to taste and add the mace.

Peel and slice the mushrooms.

Add the veal and sliced mushrooms.

Cook gently for a further 5 minutes, stirring occasionally.

Gently mix in the lemon juice and cream but do not allow the sauce to reach boiling point again.

Serve hot, garnished with chopped parsley and fringed with small pieces of toast.

Farm

PORK JELLY

Clear, savoury jellies were popular in the 19th century. Made from mutton, veal, beef or pork they would most often be served with cold meats. However, in grander households highly ornamental jellies were used to decorate the table.

This recipe for pork jelly was recorded by a Cornish woman in 1895.

Pigs feet and ears
2 blades of mace
Water for cooking
Cayenne pepper

Soak the pork in a pan of water and leave overnight.

Pour off the salt water.

Add two quarts (4 pints/ 2.25 litres/ 8 cups) of fresh water and bring to the boil.

Cook for about two hours or until tender.

Remove the meat from the pan, take out the bones and strain the meat through a muslin bag.

Discard the water and boil the meat again in half a pint (300 ml/ 1¼ cups) fresh water seasoned with mace and a little cayenne pepper.

Cook for about 15 minutes.

Pout into a mould and leave the jelly to set.

Turn out when solid.

Sow

ROAST PORK AND VEGETABLE BAKE

Serves 6

In this delicious dish the pork fat drips on to the vegetables whilst they are roasting, to crisp them.

2 lbs (900 g) belly of pork
1 lb (450 g) potatoes
1 oz (50 g) salt
8 oz (225 g) onions
1 tablespoon oil
Salt and pepper

Score the rind of the pork with a knife.

Rub the salt into the meat.

Peel the potatoes and chop them into good sized pieces.

Peel and roughly quarter the onion.

Cover the vegetables with a little oil.

Season with salt and pepper.

Place the vegetables in a roasting tin.

Put a wire tray over the vegetables and put the meat on to the tray.

Cover the top of the pork with a piece of foil to protect it during cooking.

Bake in a moderate oven for about 1½ hours or until the meat is tender.

Place the meat on to a serving dish with the crisp vegetables around it.

Serve with gravy.

Oven: 375°F/190°C Gas Mark 5

PORK COBBLER

Serves 6

In medieval times, cobblers were made with a thick dough on top and bottom. Today, the dish is generally adapted with a lighter scone-type dough on the top only - sometimes rolled out as a lid, sometimes cut out as individual rounds. The same mix is used to make fruit pies, such as damson cobbler.

1½ lbs (675 g) shoulder of pork, diced
Seasoned flour
Fat for frying
2 carrots
2 onions (medium)
2 leeks
2 oz (50 g) mushrooms
½ pint (300 ml/ 1¼ cups) chicken stock
¼ pint (150 ml/ ⅔ cup) cider
Salt and pepper
A pinch of mixed herbs

For the scone mix:
10 oz (275 g) self-raising flour
¾ teaspoon of salt
3 oz (75 g) butter or lard
About 7 fl oz (200 ml/ ¾ cup) buttermilk or fresh milk
Beaten egg or a little milk

Roll the diced meat in the seasoned flour.

Peel and chop the carrots, onions and mushrooms.

Discard the outer leaves and chop the leeks.

Fry the meat and vegetables in the hot fat.

Drain and pour into an ovenproof casserole dish.

Cover with the stock and cider.

Season to taste and add the mixed herbs.

Cover the casserole and cook in a moderate oven for 1¼ hours.

To make the cobbler scone topping:

Sieve the flour and salt into a basin.

Rub in the fat until the mixture resembles fine breadcrumbs.

Mix with sufficient milk to give a soft dough.

If liked, a large cooking apple, finely grated, may be added to the scone topping after the fat has been rubbed in and before adding the milk.

Knead lightly.

Roll out on a floured board to about ½ inch (1 cm) thickness.

Cut into shape to fit the casserole, just resting inside the dish not on the lip, or cut into rounds with a 2 inch (5 cm) cutter, placing the rounds in a tight circle on top of the meat.

Brush the topping with beaten egg, or a little milk.

Bake the pork cobbler for further 15 minutes until the scone mixture is well risen and golden brown.

Oven: 300°F/180°C Gas Mark 4
Increase to: 400°F/200°C Gas Mark 6

STAR-GAZEY PIE

Serves 4-6

This traditional Cornish dish can be made with small herrings, mackerel or pilchards. The fish are left whole and arranged so that the heads protude through the pie-crust gazing skywards, thereby giving the dish its name. This also allows the rich oil in the head of the fish to drain into the pie during cooking.

8 pilchards (or small herring or mackerel)
8 oz (225 g) breadcrumbs
Juice and grated rind of 1 lemon
2 oz (50 g) chopped parsley
2 hard-boiled eggs, chopped
2 slices of bacon, chopped
Salt and pepper
¼ pint (150 ml/ ⅔ cup) cream
8 oz (225 g) shortcrust pastry
A little milk
A little parsley to garnish

Wash, scale and remove the bones from each fish but leave the heads on.

Season the inside of the fish with salt and pepper and a little chopped parsley.

Mix the breadcrumbs with the juice and the rind of the lemon.

Grease a large pie dish.

Put a layer of breadcrumb mixture in the bottom of the dish.

Season well.

Put the fish on to the breadcrumb base so that the heads are facing upwards.

Mix the chopped egg and pieces of bacon together.

Put this mixture into the spaces between the fish.

Pour over the cream.

Roll out the pastry over the pie making slits round the head of each fish so that it is visible.

Brush the top of the pastry with a little milk and bake for about one hour.

Serve with a piece of parsley in the mouth of each fish.

Oven: 350°F/180°C Gas Mark 4

SALMON PIE

Serves 4-6

1 lb (450 g) fresh salmon (cod, haddock or hake can be used instead)
A little milk for poaching
1 bouquet garni
Salt and pepper
6 oz (175 g) cooked and peeled prawns
2 oz (50 g) butter or margarine
2 oz (50 g) flour
½ pint (300 ml/ 1¼ cups) milk
A few drops of anchovy essence
1 lb (450 g) mashed potatoes made with 2 oz (50 g) butter and a little milk
1 oz (25 g) butter
2 oz (50 g) grated cheese

Put the fish in a shallow pan with a little milk to cover and the bouquet garni.

Season with salt and pepper and poach gently until the fish is tender.

Strain and reserve the fish stock.

Remove the skin and bones and flake the fish.

Melt the butter or margarine.

Stir in the flour to make a roux.

Cook for a few moments, stirring all the time.

Gradually add the reserved fish stock and the milk, continuing to stir.

Bring to the boil and simmer until the sauce thickens.

Season with salt, pepper and achovy essence.

Add the fish and prawns to the sauce.

Put the fish mixture into a greased ovenproof dish.

Cover with mashed potatoes.

Dot with butter and bake in a moderate oven for 20-25 minutes.

Remove from the oven.

Sprinkle the top with grated cheese and put the fish under a hot grill for a few minutes until the cheese bubbles.

Oven: 375°F/190°C Gas Mark 5

TROUT PIE

An early 18th century recipe.

8 oz (225 g) shortcrust or flaky pastry
1 lb (450 g) trout
½ lb (225 g) eel
1 tablespoon fresh herbs, finely chopped (parsley, thyme, marjoram)
6 oz (175 g) Jerusalem artichoke
4 oz (100 g) mushrooms
1 tablespoon chopped capers
½ lemon sliced
1 teaspoon mixed spice
1 oz (25 g) butter

Peel the artichokes and soak in cold water.

Clean, remove the scales and fillet the trout.

Clean and skin the eel. Remove the bone and cut into 3 inch (7·5 cm) pieces.

Put the fish into a pie dish and sprinkle with the mixed herbs and spices.

Slice the artichoke and mushroom.

Add to the dish, with the chopped capers and slices of lemon.

Dot the top with butter.

Roll out the pastry on a floured board.

Cover the pie dish with the pastry, dampen the edges, and press them down firmly to seal.

Trim the pastry around the edges and decorate with a fork.

Bake in a moderately hot oven for 40-45 minutes.

Oven: 375°F/190°C Gas Mark 5

SQUAB PIE

Serves 4

Squabs are young pigeons. The Cornish sometimes used commorants in place of squabs, but they had to be skinned first as they tend to be tough. The pie can also be made with mutton, beef or veal.

8 oz (225 g) shortcrust pastry
2-3 squabs
1 large cooking apples
1 large onion
1 oz (25 g) brown sugar
Salt and pepper

Clean the squabs, joint them and place in the bottom of an ovenproof dish.

Season with salt and pepper.

Peel, core and slice the apple. Peel and slice the onion.

Put a layer of sliced apple over the meat and then a layer onion.

Sprinkle the sugar over the top.

Roll out the pastry on a floured board.

Cover the pie with a pastry lid.

Slit to make a vent.

Glaze with either a little milk or beaten egg.

Bake in a moderate oven for about one hour.

Oven: 400°F/200°C Gas Mark 6

Pidgeon

CREAMY CHICKEN, HAM AND LEEK PIE

Serves 4

Chicken pie is enjoyed throughout the country, but in Cornwall, cream is added through the air vent in the pastry lid just before serving.

A 3 lb-4 lb (1.5 kg - 1.75 kg) chicken or 4 chicken pieces
¼ lb (100 g) cooked ham
2 leeks
1½ oz (40 g) butter or margarine
1½ oz (40 g) flour
¾ pint (450 ml/ 2 cups) chicken stock
Salt and pepper
1 teaspoon mixed herbs
½ lb (225 g) puff or flaky pastry
¼ pint (150 ml/ ⅔ cup) Cornish cream or double cream
Beaten egg or milk to glaze

Strip the raw meat from the chicken bones (these can be used to make the chicken stock).

Chop the ham.

Peel and chop the leeks.

Melt the fat in a saucepan, and stir in the flour to make a roux.

Gradually stir in the chicken stock, bring to the boil, simmer stirring continually until the sauce thickens.

Season with salt and pepper to taste and add the herbs.

Mix the chicken ham and leeks into the sauce.

Put the mixure into an ovenproof dish.

Roll out the pastry on a floured board to form a lid.

Put the pastry lid on the dish decorating the edge with a fork, or as desired.

Brush the top of the pie with the beaten egg or milk.

Bake the pie in a hot oven for 10 minutes to set the pastry, then reduce to moderate and cook for a further 45 minutes.

Gently heat the cream, but do not allow it to boil.

Pour the cream through the hole in the pastry lid before serving.

Oven: 425°F/220°C Gas Mark 7
Reduce to: 350°F/180°C Gas Mark 4

RABBIT PIE

Serves 4

1 rabbit
Seasoned flour
1 lb (450 g) onions
2 carrots
8 oz (225 g) bacon
Oil and fat for frying
1 oz (25 g) parsley
1 pint (600 ml/ 2½ cups) white stock
½ lb (225 g) shortcrust pastry

Prepare and joint the rabbit.

Roll each piece in seasoned flour.

Peel and chop the onions and carrots.

Remove the rinds from the bacon, and chop.

Heat the oil or fat in a frying pan and fry the onions until soft, with the bacon. Remove.

Fry the rabbit joints until brown on all sides.

Put into a pie dish with the bacon and onions.

Chop the parsley finely and sprinkle over the rabbit, add the carrots and cover with the stock.

Roll out the pastry on a floured board.

Damp the edges of the pie dish.

Cover with the pastry, pressing down the edge firmly to seal and decorating with a fork.

Make a slit in the top of the pie for the steam to escape.

Bake in a moderate oven for 10 minutes then reduce the temperature to moderate and continue cooking for a further 40-45 minutes or until golden brown.

Oven: 400°F/200°C Gas Mark 6
Reduce to: 350°F/180°C Gas Mark 4

MUTTON AND APPLE PIE

Serves 4

1 lb (450 g) shortcrust pastry
1 lb (450 g) lean mutton
1 onion
2 large cooking apples
1 tablespoon sugar
2 oz (50 g) butter
A sprig of fresh thyme, chopped, or ½ teaspoonful dried thyme
Salt and pepper
A little good thick gravy
A little milk to glaze

Cut the mutton into small pieces removing any skin and fat.

Peel and chop the onion. Peel, core and slice the apple.

Melt the butter in a pan and fry the onion until it is transparent. Lightly fry the apple slices.

Remove the onion and apple, and fry the pieces of meat for a few minutes on each side.

Roll out half the pastry on a floured surface.

Line a greased pie dish with the pastry.

Put the meat, onion and apple in the dish.

Sprinkle with the sugar, thyme and seasoning.

Moisten with a little gravy.

Roll out the remaining pastry, and place over the pie.

Moisten the edges, press together and crimp with a fork.

Make a slit in the centre of the lid.

Brush with a little milk to glaze the top of the pastry.

Bake in a moderate oven for one hour.

Oven: 375°F/190°C Gas Mark 5

CORNISH PASTIES

It is not certain when the Cornish Pasty first originated but it was known to be eaten widely in Cornwall by the 18th century. It seems to have arisen from a need to provide hungry miners, fisherman, farmers and school children with a nourishing meal that was easily taken to the place of work where it was washed down with sweet tea. Men and boys would often take pasties on a day's hunting. The pasties could have an initial on the case to ensure it was eaten by the rightful owner. If the pasty was large, the eater would start at the opposite end to the initial so that if any was left, the pasty could easily be identified.

The style of the crimp, where the two edges of the pastry meet, varied from one area to another. The crimp also served the practical purpose of doubling as a handle so that if the eater's hands were dirty it could then be thrown away.

The pasty filling was dependant upon the availability of ingredients and the taste of the eater. Apart from meat (chuck, blade, brisket, steak or shin) ingredients such as lamb, bacon, mackerel, rabbit, broccoli, turnips, parsley, and chives were used and sweet fillings such as apple, blackberry, date and jam.

A pasty requires a good firm pastry but it should not be too rich or flaky.

All fillings are always put into the pasty uncooked in a true Cornish pasty.

Farmer

MEAT PASTY

Makes 4 Pasties

1 lb (450 g) shortcrust pastry
12 oz (350 g) chuck, blade, brisket, shin or beefsteak
6 oz (175 g) potatoes
1 onion
4 oz (100 g) turnip
Salt and pepper
A little milk to glaze

Roll out the pastry on a floured surface to about ¼ inch (5 mm) thick.

Cut into 4 equal size rounds using a small plate as a guide.

Cut the lean meat into small pieces.

Peel, chop and dice the raw potato, onion and turnip.

Mix the vegetables together and season with salt and pepper.

Divide the meat into four and place on one half of each round.

Cover with a layer of vegetables.

Fold the other half of the pastry over to form a semi circle.

Dampen the edges, shape the pasty and 'crimp' the edges together with the finger and thumb.

Repeat for each pasty.

Make a small slit with a knife in the top of each pasty.

Brush the pasties with milk and bake in a hot oven for about 15 minutes and a moderate oven for 40-45 minutes.

Oven: 425°F/220°C Gas Mark 7
Reduce to: 325°F/170°C Gas Mark 3

HERBY PASTY

Makes 4 pasties

1 lb (450 g) shortcrust pastry
4 slices of lean bacon
1 onion
8 oz (225 g) spinach
8 oz (225 g) parsley
1 egg, beaten

Prepare the pastry as before (see Meat Pasty).

Trim the rind from the bacon and cut into small pieces.

Wash and finely chop the onion.

Wash the parsley and spinach, remove the stalks and chop finely.

Add enough boiling water to cover the parsley and spinach and leave for half an hour.

Drain and sqeeze out the excess liquid.

Mix the bacon and onion with the parsley and spinach.

Add the beaten egg mixing the ingredients together well.

Put the filling into one half of each pastry round.

Fold the other half of the pastry over to form a semi circle.

Dampen the edges and 'crimp' together to seal the edges.

Repeat for each pasty.

Make a small slit with a knife at the top of each pasty.

Brush with milk and bake in a hot oven for about 15 minutes and a moderate oven for about 40 minutes.

Oven: 425°F/220°C Gas Mark 7
Reduce to: 325°F/170°C Gas Mark 3

LIKKY PASTY

Makes 4 pasties

1 lb (450 g) shortcrust pastry
2 good sized leeks
4 rashers of lean bacon
1 egg, beaten
Salt and pepper

Prepare the pastry as before (see Meat Pasty).

Wash and finely chop the leeks.

Trim the rind from the bacon and cut into small pieces.

Mix the bacon and leek together.

Add the beaten egg and seasoning.

Make the pasties as described in the previous recipe and bake in a hot oven for about 15 minutes and a moderate oven for about 40 minutes.

Oven: 425°F/220°C Gas Mark 7
Reduce to: 325°F/170°C Gas Mark 3

HAM TOAST

Serves 4

This recipe appeared in *The Guardian* in November 1890 and was recorded in a handwritten Cornish recipe.

8 oz (225 g) cooked ham, diced
1 shallot, finely chopped
1 teaspoon finely chopped parsley
½ oz (15 g) butter
2 egg yolks, beaten
2 tablespoons cream
Cayenne pepper
4 buttered toast

Heat the butter in a saucepan and when very hot gently fry the shallot.

Add the ham and stir well.

Cook for a few minutes and then add the beaten egg yolks, cream and cayenne pepper.

Stir until the mixture thickens.

Spread a little on to each piece of toast.

Sprinkle a little freshly chopped parsley over each one and serve.

Alternatively grate a little cheese on the top of each one and grill for a few minutes until the cheese bubbles.

BUTTERED EGGS

Serves 2

This early version of scrambled eggs dates from 1883.

1 oz (25 g) butter
2 eggs, beaten
Salt and pepper
2 buttered toast

Heat a little water in a saucepan.

Melt the butter in a bowl of a suitable size to sit over the heat.

Break the eggs into the bowl and stir with a wooden spoon until a good consistency.

Season with salt and pepper to taste.

Spread on hot buttered toast and serve.

POTATO CAKES

Serves 12

It was customary to cook more potatoes than was needed for a meal. The left-overs could then be used for cakes, or fried in dripping.

Savoury potato cakes with bacon, or a sweet version with sugar and currants, were often made. If the potato cakes are fried in a frying pan or on a griddle instead of baked, a lesser quantity of flour (2 oz/50 g) is used, and the suet is omitted.

8 oz (225 g) flour
8 oz (225 g) cooked, mashed potatoes
4 oz (100 g) suet
Salt and pepper
A little milk

Mix together the flour, potatoes and suet.

Season to taste.

Add a little milk if necessary to form a stiff dough.

Roll out on a floured surface.

Cut into rounds 2 inch (5 cm) across.

Place on a greased baking tray.

Bake in a hot oven for 10-15 minutes until light brown in colour.

Oven: 400°F/200°C Gas Mark 6

BROCCOLI AND BACON SUPPER DISH

Serves 3-4

1 lb (450 g) broccoli
8 oz (225 g) lean bacon rashers
1 pint (600 ml/ 2½ cups) white sauce
Salt and pepper
2 oz (50 g) grated Cheddar cheese

Cook the broccoli in boiling, salted water for about 10-15 minutes, then drain.

Remove the rinds from the bacon.

Grill the rashers until cooked.

Cut up the bacon into slices.

Put layers of broccoli and bacon in an ovenproof dish, seasoning each layer.

Pour over the white sauce.

Sprinkle the grated cheese over the top.

Put the dish under a hot grill for a few minutes until the cheese bubbles.

BROCCOLI OR CAULIFLOWER IN CHEESE SAUCE

Serves 4

A particular type of broccoli which is large, white and similar to cauliflower is grown in the West Country. In fact, cauliflowers are often called broccoli in Cornwall.

2 West Country broccoli or one large cauliflower
2 oz (50 g) butter or margarine
2 oz (50 g) flour
1 pint (600 ml/ 2½ cups) milk
5 oz (150 g) cheese
Salt and pepper

Put the prepared broccoli or cauliflower florets into boiling salted water and simmer rapidly for about 10 minutes or until soft; then strain.

Finely grate the cheese.

Melt the butter or margarine.

Stir in the flour to make a roux.

Cook, stirring all the time, for a few moments.

Continuing to stir, gradually add the milk.

Bring to the boil and simmer until the sauce thickens.

Season with salt and pepper to taste.

Add the grated cheese.

Add the cooked cauliflower to the cheese sauce, stirring gently.

Put into a pie dish and brown under a hot grill before serving, or pile on to four individual slices of bread fried in hot fat.

Excellent with sliced ham and grilled tomatoes.

CUCUMBER IN VINEGAR Serves 4

A very old Cornish recipe, still eaten today, cucumber was traditionally served with cold pork.

1 cucumber
Vinegar
Pepper

Peel the cucumber and cut into thin slices.

Lay the slices in a serving dish.

Pour over the vinegar to just cover.

Season with pepper to taste.

Leave to marinate for 2-3 hours.

BUTTERED TURNIPS Serves 3

1 lb (450 g) turnips
2 oz (50 g) butter
Salt and pepper

Peel and dice the turnips.

Melt the butter in a thick-bottomed saucepan and add the turnips.

Season with salt and pepper to taste.

Cook very slowly over a gentle heat with the lid on the saucepan, shaking occasionally to distribute the butter and seasoning, for about 45 minutes or until tender.

BLACKBERRY AND APPLE PANCAKES WITH CORNISH CLOTTED CREAM Serves 4

This is a delicious pudding made with autumn fruits. Different seasonal fruits can also be used. It is especially good with raspberries.

8 oz (225 g) plain flour
A pinch of salt
2 eggs, beaten
½ pint (300 ml/ 1¼ cups) milk
2 oz (50 g) butter for frying
8 oz (225 g) blackberries
1 large dessert apple
4 oz (100 g) Cornish clotted cream
2 oz (50 g) granulated sugar
1 tablespoon lemon juice
1 oz (25 g) caster sugar

Mix the flour and salt together. Make a well in the centre and gradually add the beaten eggs and milk.

Beat well until the mixture is free from lumps and well aerated.

Leave to stand in a cool place for about 1 hour.

Melt a little butter in a frying pan over a high heat.

When it is very hot, add a tablespoon of pancake batter.

Tilt the pan until the mixture is evenly spread over the base of the pan.

Cook for 1-2 minutes until golden brown.

Turn the pancake over and cook on the other side.

Continue until the pancake batter is finished which should make 8 pancakes.

Stack one on top of the other and keep warm.

Wash and hull the blackberries.

Peel, core and slice the apple very thinly.

Spread some of the cream over each pancake.

Cover with fruit. Sprinkle with a little sugar and lemon juice.

Fold over the pancakes and place in a ovenproof dish.

Sprinkle with a little caster sugar and grill for a few minutes.

CORNISH MINCE PIES

Makes 12

In Cornwall, mince pies were made oblong to represent the shape of the Manger. Oblong patty tins can be bought and make a change from the more traditional round shape.

For the mincemeat:
4 oz (100 g) mixed fruit
1 small apple, peeled, cored and chopped
1 oz (25 g) suet
2 oz (50 g) sugar
1 oz (25 g) mixed peel
½ oz (15 g) blanched almonds, chopped
A pinch of nutmeg
A little brandy (optional)

For the pies:
1 lb (450 g) puff or shortcrust pastry
8 oz (225 g) mincemeat
A little milk to glaze

To make the mincemeat:

Combine all the ingredients and put through a mixer.

Add a little brandy if required.

Store in a jar with a lid until needed.

To make the pies:

Roll out the pastry on a lightly floured surface.

Cut out 24 rounds with a 3 inch (8 cm) cutter.

Roll out the trimmings again to get the required number.

Grease 12 patty tins.

Line the tins with the prepared pastry rounds.

Fill each with a teaspoonful of mincemeat.

Cover with the remaining pastry rounds dampening the edges to seal.

Brush with a little milk to glaze.

Bake in a moderately hot oven for 20-25 minutes or until the pastry is golden brown.

Allow to cool in the tins before removing.

Oven: 375°F/190°C Gas Mark 5

SPICY APPLE PIE

Serves 6

1 lb (450 g) shortcrust pastry
2 lb (900 g) cooking apples
4 oz (100 g) soft brown sugar
4 oz (100 g) currants
A little lemon juice
1 teaspoon ground ginger
1 oz (25 g) caster sugar

Peel, core and slice the apples.

Roll out half the pastry on a floured surface.

Line a greased pie dish with the pastry.

Using half the apples, put a layer over the bottom of the dish.

Sprinkle with lemon juice, 2 oz (50 g) of the sugar and half the currants.

Layer the remaining apples, sprinkled with lemon juice, sugar and currants.

Finish by sprinkling the ginger over the top of the ingredients.

Roll out the second piece of pastry.

Place over the top of the dish.

Dampen the edges, press together and crimp them with a fork to decorate.

Bake in moderate oven for about 45 minutes.

When cooked dredge with caster sugar and serve hot.

Oven: 375°F/190°C Gas Mark 5

PLUM PUDDING Serves 6

'Little Jack Horner sat in the corner eating his Christmas pie, he put in his thumb and pulled out a plum and said what a good boy am I.'

Plum pudding is now more commonly known as Christmas Pudding. The original plum pudding used dried plums (prunes), and though these are not always added, the pudding retains its name. This version of a boiled plum pudding includes brandy and nutmeg.

4 oz (100 g) self-raising flour
4 oz (100 g) breadcrumbs
6 oz (175 g) suet
A pinch of salt
4 oz (100 g) soft brown sugar
12 oz (350 g) mixed fruit
1 oz (25 g) orange and citron peel
¼ teaspoon of nutmeg
2 eggs, beaten
1 tablespoon of brandy
A little milk

Mix the flour, breadcrumbs and salt together.

Add the suet and sugar, mixing well.

Stir in the mixed fruit, orange peel and nutmeg.

Add the eggs and brandy and as much milk as is needed to make a stiff batter.

Put into a greased pudding basin.

Cover with a cloth.

Steam for 3 hours.

GINGERBREAD PUDDING

Serves 6

6 oz (175 g) breadcrumbs
6 oz (175 g) suet
3 oz (75 g) plain flour
8 oz (225 g) treacle
1 egg, beaten
A teaspoonful ground ginger

Mix the breadcrumbs, suet and flour together.

Stir well until the ingredients combine.

Add the ginger.

Stir in the treacle, mixing well.

Add the egg.

Pour the mixture into a greased pudding basin.

Cover with a cloth and tie.

Steam for 2 hours.

AUNT NELLIE'S TREACLE PUDDING

Serves 4-6

3½ oz (90 g) breadcrumbs
3 oz (75 g) suet
2 oz (50 g) plain flour
2 oz (50 g) brown sugar
1 lb (450 g) treacle
2 eggs, well beaten
Grated rind and juice of a lemon

Mix together the breadcrumbs, suet and flour.

Add the sugar, stirring well.

Beat in the treacle and eggs.

Add the grated lemon rind and the juice.

Grease the pudding basin.

Pour in the mixture.

Cover with a cloth and steam for 3 hours.

FIGGIE 'OBBIN

Serves 4

Sometimes known as figgy duff. If figgie 'obbin was bought in a shop, the price sometimes depended upon how many raisins were used. 'Figs' is the Cornish for raisins and quantities of 'figs' were rarely given in the recipes, as they were hard to afford. Curranty 'obbin can be made with currants instead of raisins.

8 oz (225 g) plain flour
1 teaspoon baking powder
A pinch of salt
4 oz (100 g) suet
Raisins (about 2 oz/ 50 g - 3 oz/ 75 g)
A little grated lemon peel
Cold water to mix

Mix together the flour, baking powder, suet and salt.

Add enough water to make a stiff dough.

Roll out the pastry on a floured surface to about ½ (1 cm) inch thick.

Sprinkle the raisins and lemon peel over it.

Roll the pastry up like a swiss roll, sealing the ends.

Criss-cross the top with a knife and brush with milk.

Bake in a moderate oven for about 30 minutes.

Serve hot.

Oven: 350°F/180°C Gas Mark 4

BAKED FIGGY PUDDING

Serves 4-6

8 oz (225 g) self-raising flour
4 oz (100 g) suet
4 oz (100 g) breadcrumbs
12 oz (350 g) mixed fruit
2 oz (50 g) sugar
2 eggs, beaten
1 teaspoonful mixed spice
A pinch of salt
A little milk

Mix the flour, suet and breadcrumbs together.

Add the fruit and sugar, mixing well.

Beat in the eggs and stir in the spice and salt.

Moisten the mixture, if too dry, with a little milk.

Grease an ovenproof dish.

Pour in the mixture and bake in a cool oven for 1½-2 hours.

Oven: 300°F/150°C Gas Mark 2

Farmer Ploughs Entertainment.

TO MAKE A TANSEY

This handwritten receipt by Charity Hampton, dates from 1692. A tansy (as it is more modernly spelt) is a wild herb with yellow flowers and bitter tasting leaves often used in medicines and cookery. At that time a tansy was a popular dessert and often included apples. Recipes giving large quantities of ingredients were common because of the size of the households of the time.

Take a quart of creame and 14 eggs leaveing out six whites and halfe a pound of Naples biskets beaten very fine a little sack and as much of spinege and juice of tansey as will coller it and as much ginger as you like then mix these very well together and put it over a fire and let it boyle till it be of good thickness then butter your dish and put it on and backe it but not to much then throw some ginger and suger an orringe or two and serve it up hott.

CORNISH BURNT CREAM

Serves 6-8

1 pint (600 ml/ 2½ cups) milk
3 eggs
2 oz (50 g) sugar
1 teaspoon ground nutmeg
1 pint (600 ml/ 2½ cups) clotted cream
3 oz (75 g) caster sugar
1 lemon thinly sliced

Heat the milk in a pan over a gentle heat. Do not allow to boil.

Whisk the eggs and 2 oz (50 g) of sugar together in a basin.

Pour over the hot milk stirring all the time.

When the mixture is blended, put it into a greased ovenproof dish.

Sprinkle with the nutmeg and bake in a moderate oven for 40-45 minutes or until it is set.

Allow the baked custard to cool.

Put a layer of the custard into a greased pie dish, then spread a layer of clotted cream and continue until the dish is full.

Cover the top with slices of lemon and sprinkle generously with caster sugar.

Brown for a few minutes under the grill until the sugar is caramelized.

Oven: 325°F/160°C Gas Mark 3

CORNISH JUNKET

Serves 3-4

Junket can be served on its own, with fresh fruit, or in place of cream with desserts.

1 pint (600 ml/ 2½ cups) milk
1 oz (25 g) sugar
1 tablespoon of brandy (optional)
1½ teaspoons rennet
¼ pint (150 ml/ ⅔ cup) double cream
1 teaspoon nutmeg

Warm the milk to blood heat, about 98°F/45°C. Do not allow it to boil.

Add the sugar, and brandy if required.

Add the rennet, stirring well.

Leave to set in a warm place.

Whip the cream.

Spread evenly over the junket.

Sprinkle with nutmeg and serve.

Dairy Maid

CORNISH CLOTTED CREAM

Cornish clotted cream is generally richer, thicker and creamier in colour than Devonshire clotted cream.

2 pints (1.15 litres/ 5 cups) fresh farm whole cream milk

Strain the milk into a shallow heatproof pan.

Leave it to stand until the cream rises (about 12 hours in the summer and 24 hours in the winter).

Put the pan over a low heat.

The cream will begin to form a raised ring around the edge and then a thin layer over the top of the milk.

Remove carefully from the heat taking care that the cream layer is not disturbed.

Leave in a cool place, at least overnight.

The cream will form a crust which can then be skimmed off and put into a dish or container.

The cream, if refrigerated, will keep for up to 4 days.

Cow

BLACK CAKE

Makes a large 9 inch (23 cm) cake

An old Cornish recipe for a cake that keeps very well. It can be eaten as a plain fruit cake, or covered with almond paste and royal icing and used for a special occasion. It makes a very good Christmas cake.

Originally several cakes would be baked at one time. The cakes would be eaten during the year and after the last one was eaten a new batch of cakes would be made for the following year.

For the cake:
¼ teaspoon bicarbonate of soda
A little milk
6 oz (175 g) plain flour
½ teaspoon salt
2 oz (50 g) ground rice
4 oz (100 g) butter
4 oz (100 g) sugar
12 oz (350 g) mixed fruit or sultanas, currants and raisins
2 oz (50 g) lemon peel
1 oz (25 g) blanched almonds, chopped
½ teaspoon nutmeg
½ teaspoon cinnamon
3 eggs

For the almond paste — makes 1 lb (450 g) almond paste:
8 oz (225 g) ground almonds
4 oz (100 g) caster sugar
4 oz (100 g) icing sugar
1 egg, beaten

For the royal icing — covers a 9 inch (23 cm) round cake:
2 lb (900 g) icing sugar
4 egg whites
2 teaspoons lemon juice
1 tablespoon glycerine

To make the cake:

Dissolve the bicarbonate of soda in a little warm milk.

Sieve the flour into a basin with the salt.

Add the soda, mixing well.

Rub in the butter and work well.

Add the ground rice, mixing thoroughly.

Add the mixed fruit, lemon peel, almonds, sugar, nutmeg and cinnamon.

Combine the ingredients and add the eggs mixing well together.

Grease and line with greaseproof paper a 9 inch (23 cm) cake tin.

Pour in the mixture and bake in a slow oven for about 3½ hours.

Cover with greaseproof paper as soon as the top is brown.

Towards the end of cooking time, test with a skewer in the centre of the cake. If the skewer comes out clean, the cake is cooked.

To make the almond paste:

Mix the ground almonds and sugar together.

Make a well in the centre.

Add the egg and work to a stiff paste.

Sprinkle a surface or board with icing sugar.

Form the paste into a ball and knead lightly until smooth.

Wrap in polythene until required to prevent the paste drying.

To make the icing:

Beat the egg whites until frothy.

Gradually beat in the icing sugar.

Add the lemon juice and continue beating until the icing forms soft peaks.

Cover the bowl with a cloth and leave to stand for a few hours.

To put the paste on and ice the cake:

Spread the almond paste with a knife warmed in hot water, until it evenly covers the top of the cake. Cut away any surplus paste.

Cover the cake with half the icing.

Allow to dry and cover with the second layer of icing.

Decorate as required.

Oven: 300°F/150°C Gas Mark 2

CORNISH HEAVY CAKE

This is a scone cake which is moist inside. Heavy cakes are traditionally criss-crossed over the top which often was a job done by the children of the family.

1 lb (450 g) plain flour
¾ lb (350 g) butter
A pinch of salt
6 oz (175 g) currants
2 oz (50 g) sugar
A little cold water to mix

Divide the butter into three equal portions.

Rub one portion into the flour.

Add sufficient water to mix to a stiff dough.

Add the salt, currants and sugar mixing well.

Roll out the dough on to a floured surface.

Dot another portion of butter over the top of the dough.

Flour lightly and fold the dough.

Turn and roll the dough out again.

Repeat with the last portion of butter.

Roll out the finished dough until it is about 1 inch (2.5 cm) thick and a rectangular shape.

Criss-cross a diamond pattern with a knife over the top and brush with milk.

Bake for 30 minutes in a hot oven.

For a richer heavy cake the butter can be substituted by 1 pint (600 ml/ 2½ cups) of clotted cream and one well-beaten egg. Mix all the ingredients together, roll out and bake as before.

Oven: 425°F/220°C Gas Mark 7

SLY CAKES

Makes about 12

1 lb (450 g) flaky pastry
6 oz (175 g) currants
4 oz (100 g) chopped peel
About 3 oz (75 g) caster sugar

Roll out the pastry to a thin square or oblong on a floured board.

Mix the currants and chopped peel together.

Sprinkle the fruit over half the pastry.

Fold the other half of the pastry over the fruit.

Gently roll together.

Sprinkle the top of the pastry with the sugar.

Cut into different shapes - round, squares, oblongs as liked.

Bake for about 15 minutes in a hot oven.

Oven: 425°F/220°C Gas Mark 7

CORNISH SPILTS

Makes 18

Cornish splits are eaten warm filled with strawberry jam and clotted cream. Spilts filled with treacle and cream are known as 'thunder and lightening'.

1 lb (450 g) plain flour
½ teaspoon salt
2 oz (50 g) butter
1 oz (25 g) fresh yeast*
1 teaspoon sugar
½ pint (300 ml/ 1¼ cups) milk

Sieve the flour into a basin with the salt. Rub in the fat.

Warm the milk in a pan but do not allow it to boil.

Add the milk gradually to the flour mixture, mixing well.

Cream the yeast and sugar with a little water and set aside for a few minutes to froth.

Add the yeast and knead the dough well.

Leave the dough in the basin, cover with a floured cloth, and put in a warm place to rise for about one hour.

Put the risen dough on to a floured surface and divide into 1 inch (2.5 cm) rounds.

Flatten each one a little and place on a greased oven tray.

Cover with a floured cloth and leave for 10-15 minutes or until they have doubled in size.

Bake in a hot oven for about 20 minutes or until golden brown.

Cut the spilts in half, whilst still warm, and fill with strawberry jam and cream. Serve immediately.

Oven: 425°F/220°C Gas Mark 7

* If using dried yeast follow the manufacturer's instructions.

FAIRINGS

Makes 12

These soft ginger biscuits were made for Fairs and festive occasions. Young girls used to bake some fairings to put in a bag and give to their sweethearts.

2 oz (50 g) butter or margarine
2 tablespoons golden syrup
4 oz (100 g) self-raising flour
2 oz (50 g) caster sugar
1 teaspoon bicarbonate of soda
2 teaspoons ground ginger
1 teaspoon cinnamon
1 teaspoon mixed spice

Melt the butter and the golden syrup in a saucepan.

Sieve together the flour, sugar, bicarbonate of soda and the spices.

Stir in the butter and syrup and mix thoroughly to a stiff consistency.

Flour a working surface and your hands.

Shape the dough into small balls by hand.

Place the balls on a greased baking sheet allowing plenty of space between each one for spreading.

Bake for about 10-15 minutes or until golden brown.

Allow to cool on the tray for a few minutes before transferring to a wire rack.

Oven: 375°F/190°C Gas Mark 5

CORNISH GINGERBREAD

Makes 18

1 oz (25 g) sugar
3 oz (75 g) butter
4 oz (100 g) treacle
½ glass of brandy
8 oz (225 g) flour
A pinch of salt
1 teaspoon ginger
A few caraway seeds

Melt the butter, treacle and sugar in a saucepan.

Pour in the brandy.

Mix the flour, salt and ginger together.

Add the caraway seeds.

Stir the warm liquid into the flour and mix thoroughly.

Grease a 10 inch (25 cm) square tin and pour in the mixture.

Bake in a cool oven for about 1 hour until firm to the touch.

Oven: 300°F/150°C Gas Mark 2

POTATO CAKES FOR TEA

Makes 12

3 oz (75 g) butter
2 eggs
4 oz (100 g) caster sugar
8 oz (225 g) mashed potato
4 oz (100 g) flour
A tablespoon of brandy or to taste
A little lemon juice

Beat the butter to a cream.

Separate the egg yolks and whites and beat them.

Add them separately to the butter beating in well with the sugar.

Mix in the flour and mashed potato.

Add the brandy and lemon juice to taste.

Pour into a greased tin.

Bake in a moderate oven for about 30 minutes.

Cool and cut into large squares.

Oven: 400°F/200°C Mark 6

PORTER CAKE

An old Cornish cake that keeps well.

8 oz (225 g) plain flour
4 oz (100 g) butter
6 oz (175 g) sugar
1 egg, beaten
¼ pint (150 ml/ ⅔ cup) stout (porter)
10 oz (275 g) mixed fruit
1 teaspoon baking powder
1 teaspoon mixed spice

Melt the butter taking care not to boil.

Add the sugar and beaten egg.

Warm the stout and stir in.

Fold in the flour and baking powder.

Add the fruit and spice.

Mix ingredients well together.

Grease a 6 inch (15 cm) cake tin.

Pour in the mixture and cook in a moderate oven for 2-2½ hours.

Oven: 335°F/170°C Gas Mark 3

SIMNEL CAKE

Serves

A rich fruit cake with almond paste originally baked on Simnel Sunday — the 4th Sunday in Lent, now known as Mothering Sunday, to mark the fact that Lent was half over. Now more commonly eaten throughout England at Easter, this Simnel Cake recipe is of Cornish origin.

8 oz (225 g) plain flour
¼ oz (7 g) baking powder
8 oz (225 g) butter
8 oz (225 g) sugar
3 eggs
A little milk
8 oz (225 g) currants
2 oz (50 g) candied peel

For the paste:
2-3 oz (50-75 g) ground almonds
4 oz (100 g) caster sugar
1 egg

For the decoration:
Glacé cherries
Angelica

Cream together the butter and sugar.

Add the eggs, beating each one in separately, and fold in the flour.

Add a little milk if necessary and work to a good consistancy.

Add the currants and candied peel mixing well.

Make the almond paste by beating the ground almonds, sugar and eggs to a stiff paste.

Grease an 8 inch (20 cm) cake tin.

Put in half the cake mixture.

Spread half the almond paste over the top, and cover with the remainder of the mixture.

Bake for 45-50 minutes.

Remove the cake from the oven.

Spread the remaining almond paste over the cake and return to the oven for a few minutes until the paste melts on the cake.

Remove from the oven and whilst the paste is still soft decorate as required with glacé cherries and angelica.

Oven: 350°F/180°C Gas Mark 4

STRAWBERRY JAM

Makes 5-6 lbs

Jam is best made with small, whole strawberries. Strawberries are low in acidity and the addition of gooseberry or redcurrant juice increases the acidity and pectin needed for the setting of the jam.

2 lb (900 g) strawberries
2 lb (900 g) granulated or preserving sugar
¼ pint (150 ml/ ⅔ cup) of redcurrant or gooseberry juice

Wash and hull the strawberries and put them into a preserving pan with the juice.

Add the sugar and heat slowly until the sugar dissolves.

Bring to the boil and continue to boil gently for about 45 minutes, stirring occasionally.

Test for setting point by dipping a wooden spoon into the jam. As the jam on the spoon cools, it should begin to set.

Continue boiling if necessary until setting point is reached.

Leave the jam to cool for about 10 minutes.

Stir before putting the jam into clean 1 lb (450 g) jars.

This will prevent the fruit from rising.

Cool and cover with jam covers.

Ripe Strawberries

APPLE AND DATE CHUTNEY

Makes about 3½ lbs (1.5 kg)

1 lb (450 g) apples
1 lb (450 g) stoned dates
1 large onion
2 red chillies
8 oz (225 g) sultanas
12 oz (350 g) brown sugar
1 teaspoon dry mustard
1 teaspoon ground ginger
1 teaspoon salt
3 pints (1.75 litres/ 7½ cups) vinegar

Peel, core and chop the apples.

Peel and chop the onion.

Chop the chillies and dates.

Put into a large heavy pan with the sultanas, sugar, mustard ginger and salt.

Add the vinegar and bring to the boil.

Cover the pan and simmer for about an hour or until the mixture is thick and the ingredients tender.

Put into clean, dry jars and cover when cool.

FENNEL SAUCE

Makes about 1 pint (600 ml/ 2½ cups)

Fennel sauce is popular with mackerel but is also ideal with other fish, especially salmon.

2 oz (50 g) fresh fennel
2 oz (50 g) butter
2 oz (50 g) plain flour
1 pint (600 ml/ 2½ cups) milk
Salt and cayenne pepper
1 tablespoon lemon juice
1 tablespoon cream

Melt the butter in a pan over a low heat.

Stir in the flour and make into a roux.

Remove from the heat and gradually stir in the milk.

When the sauce is smooth, season with salt and cayenne pepper. Add a little lemon juice and return to the heat.

Stir until the sauce thickens.

Finely chop the fennel.

Stir into the sauce with the cream.

Heat gently and serve.

CIDER SAUCE

Makes 1 pint (600 ml/ 2½ cups)

½ pint (300 ml/ 1¼ cups) dry cider
1 bay leaf
Salt and pepper
2 oz (50 g) butter
2 oz (50 g) flour
1 pint (600 ml/ 2½ cups) stock

Put the cider in a saucepan.

Add the bay leaf and salt and pepper.

Bring to the boil, cover and simmer until the liquid is reduced by half.

Melt the butter in a pan.

Make a brown roux by stirring in the flour and cooking over a low heat until the roux darkens.

Remove from the heat and gradually stir in the stock and cider until the sauce is free from lumps.

Season with salt and pepper.

Bring back to the boil and simmer, stirring continuously, until reduced by a third.

Strain, adjust the seasoning and serve hot.

Saucepan

BLACKBERRY SYRUP

Blackberry syrup is delicious with ice-cream or desserts. It can be diluted with cold or hot water to make a summer or winter drink. The syrup keeps well but can be used immediately.

2 lbs (900 g) blackberries
3-4 tablespoons water
4 cloves
2 oz (50 g) root ginger
1 lb-1½ lbs (450 g - 657 g) sugar to every pint (600 ml/ 2½ cups) of juice according to taste

Place the washed fruit in a pan.

Add the water, bring to the boil and simmer gently for about 10 minutes.

Mash the fruit with a wooden spoon to a pulp.

Put the pulp into a jelly bag and squeeze out the juice.

Return the juice to the pan and add the sugar.

Stir over a low heat until the sugar dissolves.

Tie the root ginger in a muslin bag and add to the liquid with the cloves.

Bring to the boil for 10 minutes then remove from the heat and take out the spices.

Strain and bottle whilst still hot.

Sterilize the corks or stoppers by boiling in water for 10 minutes.

Put the syrup in the clean, sterilized bottles.

Fill the bottle with syrup allowing 2 inches (5 cm) space between the syrup and the stopper.

BRANDY AND RHUBARB CORDIAL

Makes about 1¾ pint (1 litre/ 4½ cups)

1¾ pints (1 litre/ 4¼ cups) brandy
4 oz (100 g) rhubarb
8 oz (225 g) plum raisins
¼ oz (7 g) liquorice root
¼ oz (7 g) lemon peel
¼ oz (7 g) fennel seed
A pinch of coriander seed
¼ oz (7 g) saffron
A few drops of cochineal

Wash the rhubarb and cut it into thin strips.

Stone and slice the plum raisins.

Slit the liquorice root and cut it into thin strips.

Put the brandy into a stone bottle with a cork.

Add the rhubarb, plum raisins, liquorice, lemon peel, fennel, coriander seed, saffron and cochineal.

Let it stand in a warm place for a fortnight.

Shake the bottle from time to time.

After two weeks strain the brandy and bottle for use.

MRS BOILAY'S BEEF TEA

Makes about 1½ pints (900 ml/ 3¾ cups)

Beef tea is ideal nourishment for the ill or convalescent. It is also a very tasty drink which can be stored in the refrigerator and used as required. This recipe is dated 1888.

1 lb (450 g) shin of beef
1½ pints (900 ml / 3¾ cups) water
Salt and pepper

Remove all the fat and gristle from the meat and cut it into very small chunks.

Soak the beef in the cold water with a pinch of salt for two hours.

Boil the meat in the same water and simmer for two and half hours or until it is cooked.

Strain the tea which is now ready for use.

The meat can be used with potatoes, vegetables and gravy or used as a pie filling.

EGGY'OT Makes about 1 pint (600 ml/ 2½ cups)

A warming drink made with beer and eggs. A nourishing drink for the elderly or convalescent can be made in the same way and substituting milk for beer.

1 pint (600 ml/ 2½ cups) ale or strong beer
2 eggs, beaten
A little sugar to taste

Warm the beer in a pan.

Beat the eggs into the beer.

Add a little sugar to taste.

Drink hot.

MAHOGANY Makes about 1 pint (600 ml/ 2½ cups)

A rich drink drunk by Cornish fishermen.

1 pint (600 ml/ 2½ cups) gin
½ pint (300 ml/ 1¼ cups) treacle

Mix together.

Beat well and serve.

METHEGLIN OR SPICED MEAD

Makes about 2 pints (1.15 litres/ 5 cups)

Metheglin has been a popular drink in Cornwall for centuries and is often served hot. It is similar to the renowned Cornish mead which is believed to have been drunk by King Arthur and the Knights of the Round Table at a gathering in Tintagel, North Cornwall, in the 12th century.

1 lb (450 g) honey
2 pints (1.15 litres/ 5 cups) water
½ oz (15 g) root ginger, preferably Jamaican
¼ oz (7 g) yeast

Boil the water for 15 minutes.

Put in the honey and simmer for an hour.

Skin off any scum from the top.

Cut up the ginger, bruise it and put it in a muslin bag, tied at the top.

Put the muslin bag in the liquid.

Allow to cool.

When almost cold, add the yeast.

Bottle and leave in a warm place such as an airing cupboard until fermentation is complete.

Bottle and cork when it is completely clear.

The longer it is left before drinking the better. Allow at least 12 months and up to 3 years for the flavour to improve.

SPRUCE

Makes 2 pints (1.15 litres/5 cups)

An old Cornish drink taken at harvest time.

4 oz (100 g) sugar
¼ teaspoon tartaric acid
A pinch of ground ginger
1-2 tablespoons lemon juice to taste
2 pints water

Bring about 8 tablespoons of the water to boil.

Dissolve the sugar in the hot water.

Add the lemon juice, tartaric acid and ground ginger stirring well.

Dilute with the remaining water.

Serve chilled with ice and slices of lemon.

The Most Admirable Beauty Wash that was ever known...

Take a gallon of white wine, eight pints of snails, a good leg of veal, six pints of rosemary flowers if you can get them, a handful of balm, a handful or two of linseed, four lemons, a quart of cream. Cut your veal in small pieces: break all the bones: wipe the snails very clean and crack them. Pare the lemons and slice them. Shred the balm, bruise the seeds. So put them all together in the white wine and distil them — this quantity will very well yield four quarts of water: when it is stilled you may put to every quart a dram of prepared pearl. you must bury it a month to fetch out the fire. Put in every bottle a leaf of gold to keep it.

You must give the snails for 4 or 5 days talc in powder with fennel to eat. This will make them very fat. You must take them out of the shells and wipe them clean.

This wash a lady used till she was 80 years of age and it preserved the skin of her face to look as young and smooth as a girl of fifteen. It is believed who ever useth this can never look old.

Acknowledgements:

Grateful thanks are extended to the many people of Cornwall who have contributed towards this collection of recipes, including:

Cornwall County Museum, Truro, for:
Charity Hampton's Tansey
Beauty Wash
Facts from *The Royal Cornwall Gazette and News*

Cornish Studies Library, Redruth, for:
Buttered Eggs
Chicken Cream
Ham Toast
Pork Jelly
Gingerbread Pudding
Fish Balls
Aunt Nellie's Treacle Pudding
Mrs Boilay's Beef Tea 1888

Geoff and Jane Sobey for:
Spider Crab Supper
Cucumber in Vinegar

Cynthia Stamford for valuable books for research.